Growing Things

Plant Plumbing

A Book About Roots and Stems

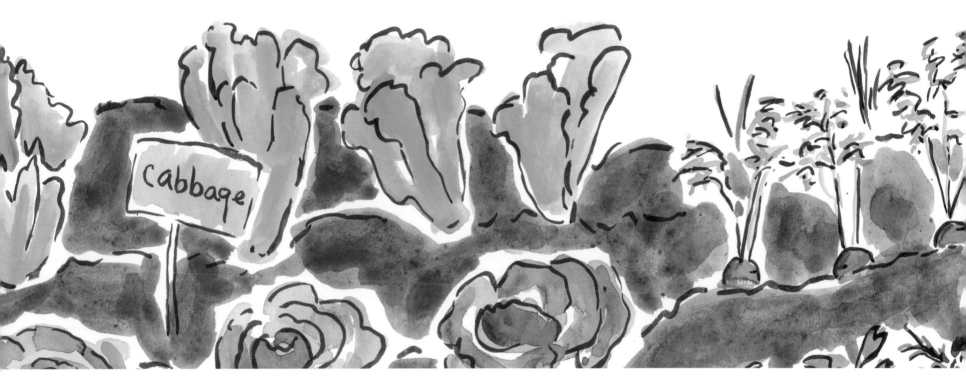

cabbage

Written by Susan Blackaby

Illustrated by Charlene DeLage

Content Adviser: Jeffrey H. Gillman, Ph.D., Assistant Professor
Horticultural Science, University of Minnesota, St. Paul, Minnesota

Reading Adviser: Susan Kesselring, M.A., Literacy Educator
Rosemount-Apple Valley-Eagan (Minnesota) School District

PICTURE WINDOW BOOKS
Minneapolis, Minnesota

D1262377

Editor: Nadia Higgins
Designer: Nathan Gassman
Page production: Picture Window Books
The illustrations in this book were painted with watercolor.

Picture Window Books
1710 Roe Crest Drive
North Mankato, MN 56003
www.capstonepub.com

Library of Congress Cataloging-in-Publication Data
Blackaby, Susan.
Plant plumbing : a book about roots and stems / written by Susan Blackaby ; illustrated by Charlene DeLage.
v. cm. — (Growing things)
Contents: Plant parts—Under the ground—Two kinds of roots—What stems do—Inside a stem—All sorts of
stems—Potato print wrapping paper—Fun facts—Water up a stem.
ISBN-13: 978-1-4048-0109-7 (hardcover) ISBN-10: 1-4048-0109-X (hardcover)
ISBN-13: 978-1-4048-0385-5 (softcover) ISBN-10: 1-4048-0385-8 (softcover)
1. Roots (Botany)—Juvenile literature. 2. Stems (Botany)—Juvenile literature. [1. Roots (Botany) 2. Stems
(Botany)] I. DeLage, Charlene, 1944- ill. II. Title.
QK644 .B59 2003
575.5'4—dc21
2002156331

Printed in the United States of America in North Mankato, Minnesota.
092011
006367R

Table of Contents

Plant Parts   4

Under the Ground   6

Two Kinds of Roots   10

What Stems Do   12

Inside a Stem   14

All Sorts of Stems   16

Potato Print Wrapping Paper   22

Fun Facts   22

Water Up a Stem   23

Words to Know   23

To Learn More   24

Index   24

Plant Parts

Take a close look at a plant.

Bright flowers and green leaves catch your eye.

mums

cabbage

4

Look again. What does the plant's stem look like?

Can you see any roots? Roots and stems are important plant parts, too.

5

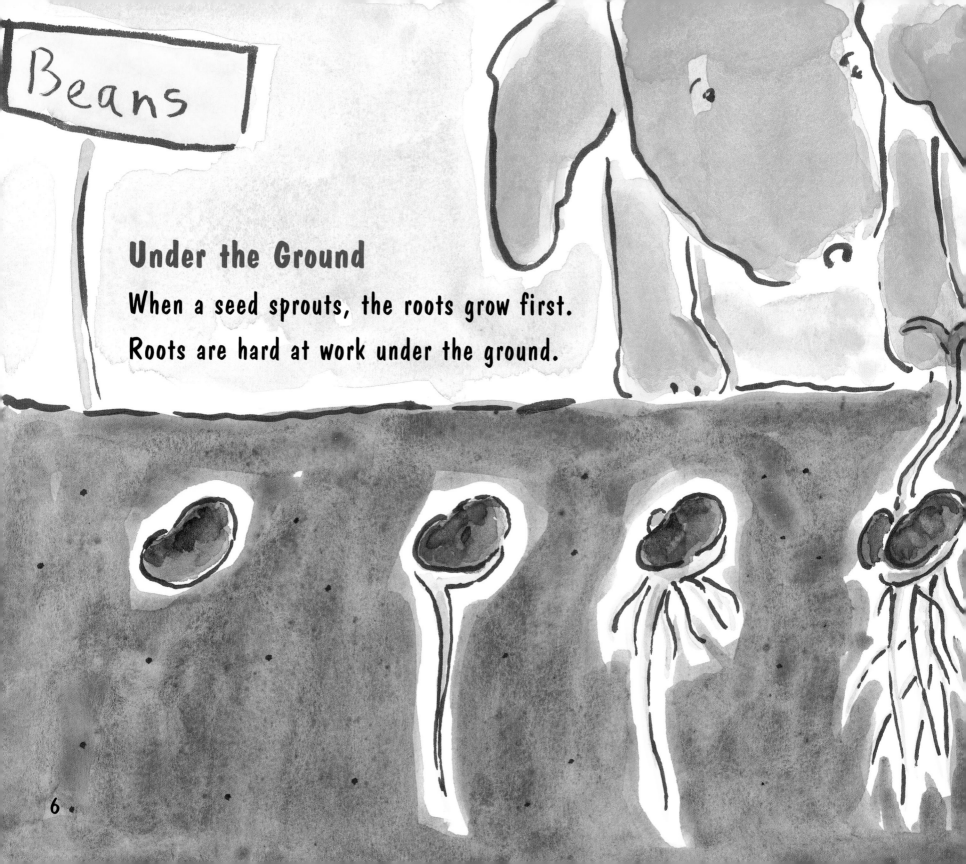

Beans

Under the Ground

When a seed sprouts, the roots grow first.
Roots are hard at work under the ground.

6

Roots have four jobs.
- Roots help keep the plant in the ground.
- Roots soak up water and nutrients in the soil.
- Roots help hold up the plant.
- Roots store food for the plant to use.

7

Roots do their jobs best in loose, crumbly soil. Loose soil has lots of holes. The holes hold air and water that roots need to stay healthy. Loose soil lets roots spread out and grow strong.

Some roots store high-energy food.
The food that helps the plant grow can help you grow, too.

Things You Dig to Eat:
- Carrots
- Radishes
- Turnips
- Beets

Two Kinds of Roots

Some plants have a fat main root called a tap root.

It grows straight down into the soil. A carrot is a tap root.

Some plants have stringy little roots that spread out under the ground.
These roots do not have to go very deep to find what they need.

What Stems Do

Once the roots take hold in the ground, a seedling sprouts. The stem pushes up into the sunlight. The stem is the part of the plant that has leaves, buds, and nodes.

A bud is the start of a leaf, a flower, or a branch.
Buds are found at the ends of stems.
They are also found at bulges along the stem called nodes.

Most stems grow up from the ground.

Stems called runners trail along the ground.

New plants take root from nodes along the runner.

Inside a Stem

A stem is like a bundle of straws. Some straws carry food up the stem. Water and nutrients soaked up by the roots move up to the leaves. Some straws carry food down the stem.

Food made in the leaves gets sent down to the roots.

All Sorts of Stems

Some stems grow underground.

Underground stems store food for the plant, just like roots do.

A potato is an underground stem.
Its eyes are the buds.

Some stems are soft and green.

They can bend without breaking.

Flowers, vegetables, and houseplants have soft stems.

Some stems are woody and hard.
They do not bend like soft stems do.
A tree trunk is a big, woody stem.

A shoot is a baby stem with new leaves.
A twig is a new stem with no leaves.
A branch is an old stem.

19

In the fall, some plants stop making food and lose their leaves.
Soft stems die, but the roots are still alive.
Woody stems stand bare through the cold winter.

In the spring, plants use food stored in the roots to start growing again. New soft stems grow up from the ground. Woody stems come to life. Green leaves and fat flower buds tell you winter is over.

Potato Print Wrapping Paper

You will need:
- a grown-up to help you
- a potato
- a butter knife
- paint or inkpads
- big sheets of white paper

Follow these steps to make potato print wrapping paper.

1. Cut the potato in half. Carve a design into the white, flat part of the potato with the butter knife. Keep in mind that the part of the design that prints is the part that sticks up. (Handy tip: If you carve letters, be sure to make them backwards on the potato.)

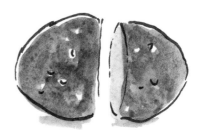

2. Stamp the potato in the paint or on the inkpad.

3. Use the potato to print a design on the paper.

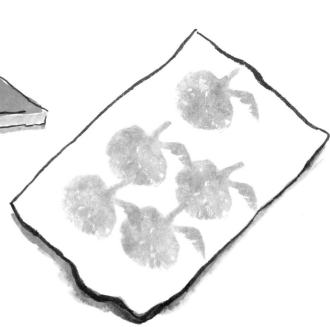

Fun Facts

- Most trees have small roots that branch off of one big tap root.

- If there is enough water, the roots of a very big tree do not need to grow more than 3 or 4 feet (1 to 1H meters) deep.

- A new plant can grow from a piece of a stem that has a bud or a node.

- Celery and asparagus are stems that you can eat.

Water Up a Stem

Have a grown-up set up this experiment so that you can see how water travels up a stem.

1. Slice the end off of a celery stick.
2. Put an inch or two (3 to 6 centimeters) of water in a glass. Mix in two to three drops of red food coloring. Set the cut end of the celery stalk in the glass.
3. Put the glass on a windowsill.
4. Wait one day.
5. Take the celery out of the glass. Wash off the end. Have a grown-up slice the stalk into six pieces. See the red dots where the water has been carried up the stem!

Words to Know

bud—a swelling on the stem that will grow into a flower, leaf, or branch

node—a bulge on the stem where a bud is attached

nutrients—parts of food, like vitamins, that are used for growth

seedling—a young plant

soil—another word for dirt

To Learn More

More Books to Read

Fowler, Allan. *Taking Root*. New York: Children's Press, 2000.

Saunders-Smith, Gail. *Stems*. Mankato, Minn.: Pebble Books, 1998.

Schwartz, David M. *Plant Stems and Roots*. Milwaukee, Wis.: Gareth Stevens, 2000.

Whitehouse, Patricia. *Roots*. Chicago: Heinemann Library, 2002.

On the Web

FactHound offers a safe, fun way to find Web sites related to topics in this book. All of the sites on FactHound have been researched by our staff.

1. Visit www.facthound.com
2. Type in this special code: 140480109X
3. Click on the FETCH IT button.

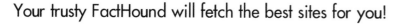

Your trusty FactHound will fetch the best sites for you!

Index

air, 8

bud, 12, 17, 21, 22

flowers, 4, 12, 18, 21

leaves, 4, 12, 15, 19, 20–21

nodes, 12–13, 22

nutrients, 7, 14

roots, 5, 6, 14–15, 20–21, 22
    and soil, 8, 10
    edible roots, 9
    kinds of, 10–11
    purpose, 7, 9

seed, 6

seedling, 12

stems, 5, 12, 20–21, 22, 23
    carrying food, 14–15
    kinds of, 13, 16–19

sunlight, 12

water, 8, 14, 22, 23

24